First Time

Going to School

Melinda Radabaugh

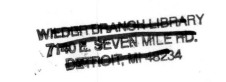
Heinemann Library
Chicago, Illinois

Designed by Sue Emerson, Heinemann Library
Printed and bound in the United States by Lake Book Manufacturing, Inc.

07 06 05 04 03
10 9 8 7 6 5 4 3 2 1

Library of Congress Cataloging-in-Publication Data
Radabaugh, Melinda Beth.
   Going to school / Melinda Beth Radabaugh.
      p. cm. -- (First time)
   Includes index.
   ISBN 1-4034-0227-2 (HC), 1-4034-0466-6 (Pbk.), 1-4034-3814-5 (BB)
   1. Schools--Juvenile literature. 2. School day--Juvenile literature. [1. Schools. 2. First day of school.]
   I. Title. II. Series.
   LB1513 .R33 2002
   372.12'44--dc21

2001008298

Acknowledgments
The author and publishers are grateful to the following for permission to reproduce copyright material:
pp. 4, 6, 7, 9, 11, 13B, 14, 15, 17 Brian Warling/Heinemann Library; p. 5 Jay Thomas/Image State; p. 8 Carolee Biddle/Heinemann Library; pp. 10, 18, 19 Greg Williams/Heinemann Library; p. 12 Nancy Sheehan/Index Stock Imagery, Inc.; p. 13T Robert Llewellyn/Image State; p. 16L Robert Lifson/Heinemann Library; p. 16R David Schmidt/Masterfile; p. 20 Richard Hutchings/Corbis; p. 21 Tony Greeman/Photo Edit; p. 22 (row 1) PhotoDisc; p. 22 (row 2) PhotoDisc; p. 22 (row 3, L-R) RDF/Visuals Unlimited, Greg Williams/Heinemann Library; p. 23 (row 1, L-R) Greg Williams/Heinemann Library, Brian Warling/Heinemann Library, Brian Warling/Heinemann Library; p. 23 (row 2, L-R) EyeWire Collection/ Getty Images, Spencer Grand/PhotoEdit, Inc., Thomas A. Heinz/Corbis, p. 23 (row 3, L-R) Greg Williams/Heinemann Library, Catherine Karnow/Corbis, Greg Williams/Heinemann Library; p. 23 (row 4, L-R) Brian Warling/Heinemann Library, Robert Lifson/Heinemann Library, Carolee Biddle/Heinemann Library; p. 24 (L-R) PhotoDisc, PhotoDisc, Greg Williams/Heinemann Library; back cover (L-R) Robert Lifson/Heinemann Library, Brian Warling/Heinemann Library

Cover photograph by Brian Warling/Heinemann Library
Photo research by Amor Montes de Oca

Every effort has been made to contact copyright holders of any material reproduced in this book. Any omissions will be rectified in subsequent printings if notice is given to the publisher.

Special thanks to our advisory panel for their help in the preparation of this book:
Eileen Day, Preschool Teacher
Chicago, IL

Ellen Dolmetsch,
Library Media Specialist
Wilmington, DE

Kathleen Gilbert,
Second Grade Teacher
Round Rock, TX

Sandra Gilbert,
Library Media Specialist
Houston, TX

Angela Leeper,
Educational Consultant
North Carolina Department
of Public Instruction
Raleigh, NC

Pam McDonald,
Reading Support Specialist
Winter Springs, FL

Melinda Murphy,
Library Media Specialist
Houston, TX

We would also like to thank the teachers, staff, and students at Stockton Elementary School in Chicago, Illinois, for their help with this book.

Some words are shown in bold, **like this.**
You can find them in the picture glossary on page 23.

Contents

Why Do You Go to School?

You go to school to learn.

You can learn to read and count.

You can learn to share with friends.

You can have fun at school.

What Kinds of Schools Are There?

Some schools are in a school building.

Some are at **churches, temples,** or **mosques.**

Some schools have children of all ages.

Other schools have only young children.

When Do You Go to School?

Most children go to school on **weekdays.**

There is no school on Saturday or Sunday.

Some children stay at school all day.

Other children go only part of
a day.

Where Is Your School?

Schools can be near your home.

Some children walk to school.

Schools can be far away.

Some children ride to school on a **school bus.**

What Do You Do at School?

At school, you listen to the teacher.

You do school work.

You can paint.

You can play with blocks, too.

What Do You Eat at School?

You can eat breakfast at some schools.

Sometimes there is a morning snack.

You can eat lunch at school.

You can bring your lunch or buy it.

Who Works at a School?

principal

teacher

The **principal** works in the school office.

Teachers work in classrooms.

librarian

custodians

A **librarian** works in the **library**.

Custodians take care of the building.

What Do You Need for School?

A **backpack** holds your papers and books.

Sometimes you bring a toy to show your class.

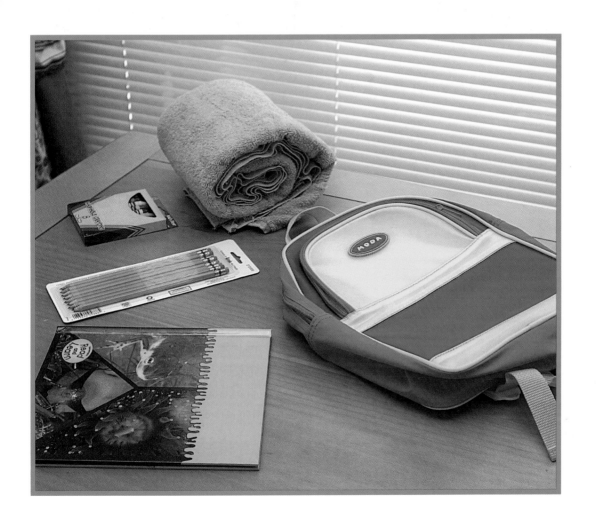

You might need **crayons** and pencils.

You might take a **towel** for a nap.

What Happens at the End of the Day?

You clean up.

You put your things in your **backpack**.

Then, you go home.

Will you go to your house
or a friend's?

Quiz

What goes in your **backpack?**

Look for the answers on page 24.

Picture Glossary

backpack
pages 18,
20, 22

librarian
page 17

school bus
page 11

church
page 6

library
page 17

temple
page 6

crayons
page 19

mosque
page 6

towel
page 19

custodians
page 17

principal
page 16

| Monday |
| Tuesday |
| Wednesday |
| Thursday |
| Friday |

weekday
page 8

23

Note to Parents and Teachers

Reading for information is an important part of a child's literacy development. Learning begins with a question about something. Help children think of themselves as investigators and researchers by encouraging their questions about the world around them. Each chapter in this book begins with a question. Read the question together. Look at the pictures. Talk about what you think the answer might be. Then read the text to find out if your predictions were correct. Think of other questions you could ask about the topic, and discuss where you might find the answers. Assist children in using the picture glossary and the index to practice new vocabulary and research skills.

Index

Answers to quiz on page 22

| crayons | scissors | pencils |

Charts and Graphs

Heather C. Hudak
and James Duplacey

WEIGL PUBLISHERS INC.

New York, NY 10118-0069

Website: www.weigl.com

Library of Congress Cataloging-in-Publication Data

Hudak, Heather C., 1975-
   Charts and graphs / Heather C. Hudak and James Duplacey.
       p. cm. -- (Social studies essential skills)
   Includes index.
   ISBN 978-1-59036-759-9 (library binding : alk. paper) -- ISBN 978-1-59036-760-5 (soft cover : alk. paper)
   1. Social sciences--Study and teaching (Elementary)--Charts, diagrams, etc. 2. Graphic methods--Study and teaching (Elementary) I. Duplacey, James. II. Title.
   H62.2.H83 2007
   372.83--dc22
                                 2007024011

Printed in the United States of America
1 2 3 4 5 6 7 8 9 0 11 10 09 08 07

Editor: Heather C. Hudak
Design: Terry Paulhus

Table of Contents

Learning about Charts and Graphs

Charts and graphs are **graphic organizers**. They both show information in a visual way. Charts and graphs use drawings or tables to compare quantities. Often, they are easier to read than the information they are comparing. Most show the relationship between two or more changing items or **variables**. Charts and graphs differ in the way they display or show information.

Comparing Redwood Trees

	Dawn Redwood	**Giant Sequoia**	**Coast Redwood**
Height	to 100 feet (30.5 m)	to 311 feet (94.8 m)	to 367.8 feet (112.1 m)
Base	to 8 feet (2.4 m) in diameter	to 30 feet (9.1 m) in diameter	to 22 feet (6.7 m) in diameter
Age	to 4,000 years	to 3,200 years	to 2,000 years

Charts often use boxes placed in columns and rows. They show how items in one column or box relate to the items in another. Charts sometimes use words and different colors to help present the data.

Comparing the Height of Redwood Trees

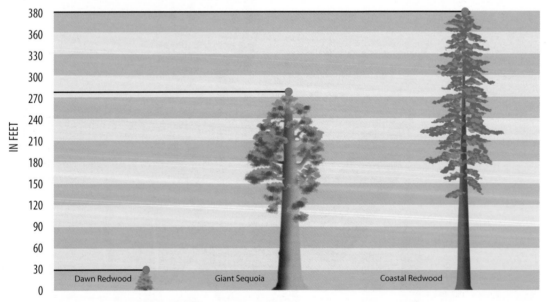

Graphs often use images, lines, or bars to show information. These lines are made by plotting and connecting points on a grid. A grid is made up of horizontal and vertical lines. Each point on the grid is used to compare two types of data.

Is it a Chart or a Graph?

Look at the following examples. Which are charts? Which are graphs?
How are they different? How are they similar?

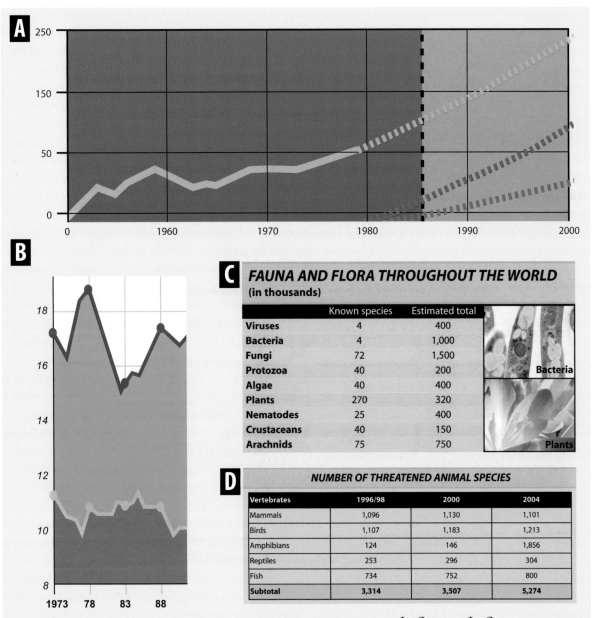

A

B

C FAUNA AND FLORA THROUGHOUT THE WORLD
(in thousands)

	Known species	Estimated total
Viruses	4	400
Bacteria	4	1,000
Fungi	72	1,500
Protozoa	40	200
Algae	40	400
Plants	270	320
Nematodes	25	400
Crustaceans	40	150
Arachnids	75	750

Bacteria

Plants

D NUMBER OF THREATENED ANIMAL SPECIES

Vertebrates	1996/98	2000	2004
Mammals	1,096	1,130	1,101
Birds	1,107	1,183	1,213
Amphibians	124	146	1,856
Reptiles	253	296	304
Fish	734	752	800
Subtotal	3,314	3,507	5,274

Answers: A.) graph B.) graph C.) chart D.) chart

Recognizing a Chart

Charts use visual cues, such as words and pictures, to show information. Some charts are large and can be displayed on a wall. Others are small and can be found on the page of a book. Charts may use bright colors and different shapes and symbols to help the reader understand the information that is being presented.

*Look at the chart on this page. It shows how different types of **cetaceans** are grouped. The top of the chart shows the group that these animals all belong to. The group is divided into two main types—toothed whales and **baleen** whales. These remaining boxes show which whales, dolphins, and porpoises belong to each of these two types.*

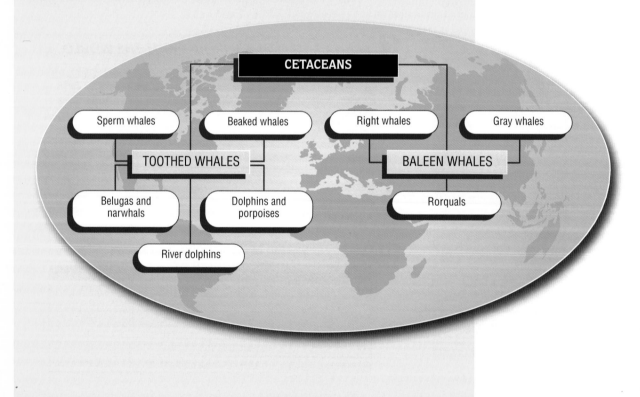

SOCIAL STUDIES ESSENTIAL SKILLS

Reading a Chart

Charts are easy to read. They may use symbols to help you understand the information that is being shown.

Some charts have a legend to show what each symbol means. By looking at the legend and the columns or symbols on the chart, you can learn what information the chart is presenting.

Find all the symbols on this chart. Then, go to the legend to find out what each symbol means. Do they help you understand the chart?

THE PROCESS FOR BUYING A SHIRT

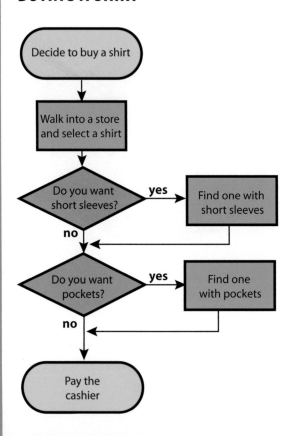

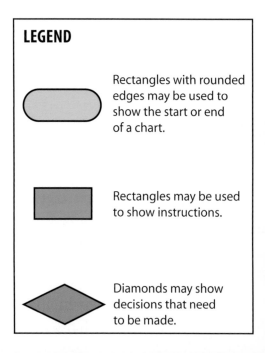

LEGEND

Rectangles with rounded edges may be used to show the start or end of a chart.

Rectangles may be used to show instructions.

Diamonds may show decisions that need to be made.

Knowing Types of Charts

Flow Charts

Flow charts show the order of events or steps in a process. They also show how the steps work in relation to each other. Flow charts use special symbols to show the steps in the process. Squares, circles, diamonds, and rectangles are common symbols. Arrows often show the connection between items on the chart. A flow chart might show the order for writing a book report.

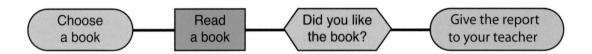

Pie Charts

Pie charts are shaped like a circle or a pie. The pie has lines, or "slices," to show the different types of information that are being presented. The circle is cut into pieces of different sizes. Each piece is a percentage of the whole. When added together, the total equals 100 percent. A pie chart might show how much of the world's water is drinkable fresh water.

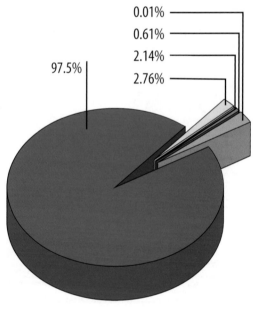

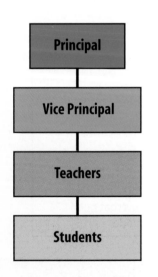

Organizational Charts

Organizational charts show who is in charge of each section or department within a company or organization. An organizational chart for your school would show the principal at the top. Below the principal would be the vice-principals, the teachers, and the students.

Identifying the Chart

There are three different kinds of charts printed below. Can you identify them? Which one is a pie chart? Which one is a flow chart? Which one is an organizational chart?

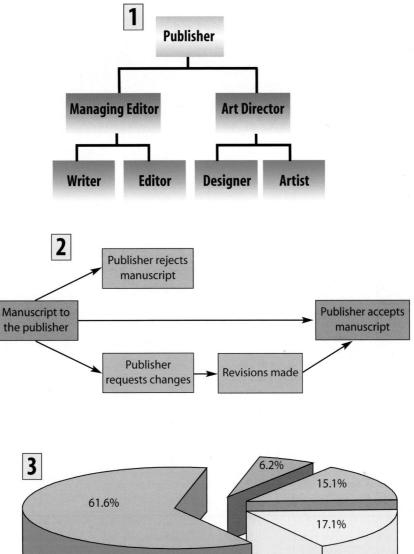

Using Charts

Charts are used to show information in a clear and accurate way. Similar types of **data** can be grouped together in rows or in columns. Rows and columns can be color-coded to show that they contain information that is related. Charts can be used to attract and hold attention, develop an idea, present information to small groups, highlight key points or ideas, and review and preview material.

PLANET FEATURES

PLANET	Distance from the Sun	Days to Orbit the Sun	Diameter	Length of Day	Average Temperature
Mercury	36 million miles (58 million km)	88	3,032 miles (4,880 km)	4,223 hours	333° Fahrenheit (167° C)
Venus	67 million miles (108 million km)	225	7,521 miles (12,104 km)	2,802 hours	867° Fahrenheit (464° C)
Earth	93 million miles (150 million km)	365	7,926 miles (12,756 km)	24 hours	59° Fahrenheit (15° C)
Mars	142 million miles (229 million km)	687	4,222 miles (6,975 km)	25 hours	−81° Fahrenheit (−63° C)
Jupiter	484 million miles (779 million km)	4,331	88,846 miles (142,984 km)	10 hours	−230° Fahrenheit (−146° C)
Saturn	891 million miles (1,434 million km)	10,747	74,897 miles (120,535 km)	11 hours	−285° Fahrenheit (−176° C)
Uranus	1,785 million miles (2,873 million km)	30,589	31,763 miles (51,118 km)	17 hours	−355° Fahrenheit (−215° C)
Neptune	2,793 million miles (4,495 million km)	59,800	30,775 miles (49,528 km)	16 hours	−355° Fahrenheit (−215° C)

Making a Chart

Make a chart to list your favorite types of books and the number of each type you have read. First, make a list of your favorite books. Then, divide the books into categories, such as fiction, science fiction, non-fiction, and biographies. Then, make a chart using the information you have gathered. Color the columns for each category a different color.

Other Types of Charts

Venn Diagrams

Venn diagrams are made up of two or more overlapping or connecting circles. They are often used to show relationships between sets of things.

The two outer circles of a Venn diagram contain different information. The inner circle contains information that is common to both circles. One circle could show the number of animals that live in water. The other circle could show the number of animals that live on land. The inner circle, where the other circles overlap, would show the number of animals that live on land and in the water.

WATER ANIMALS
Dolphins
Salmon
Sharks
Tuna
Manta Rays

ANIMALS
Sea Lions
Frogs
Polar Bears
Alligators
Ducks

LAND ANIMALS
Giraffes
Dogs
Monkeys
Sparrows
Zebras

Flip Charts

Flip charts provide information to groups of people in a room or a meeting. They are a collection of large pages that are bound together at the top. The pages are then "flipped" or turned over as they are used. Each page of the chart has a different piece of information, which is written in large letters so everyone in the room can read it.

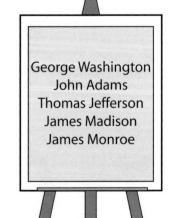

George Washington
John Adams
Thomas Jefferson
James Madison
James Monroe

Making a Venn Diagram

Make your own Venn diagram. First, do some research about two people you admire, such as President Bush and President Clinton.

Write down the ways these two people are similar and the ways they are different. For example, what college did they go to? Did they serve in the army? What did they do before they became president? Did they play sports in college? First, draw two circles that overlap. Label one circle "Bush" and the other "Clinton." In the area where the circles meet, list all the things the two men have in common. Then, write down all the ways they are different in the proper circle. Try to find at least five items to put in each section.

President of the
United States

GEORGE W. BUSH
Republican
Former Governor of Texas

BILL CLINTON
Democrat
Former Governor of Arkansas

Recognizing a Graph

Graphs are drawings or diagrams that show how numbers or amounts relate to each other. On a graph, numbers are used to show patterns. Many types of graphs have a series of points drawn on a grid. The grid has two **axes**. The x-axis runs horizontally, or from side-to-side, across the graph. The y-axis runs vertically, or from top to bottom. The place where the two axes meet is called the origin. It has a numerical value of zero.

Values are plotted along both the x- and y-axis. Points are marked at different values. Each point has a value on both the x-axis and the y-axis. The place where the point meets on both axes is called the coordinate.

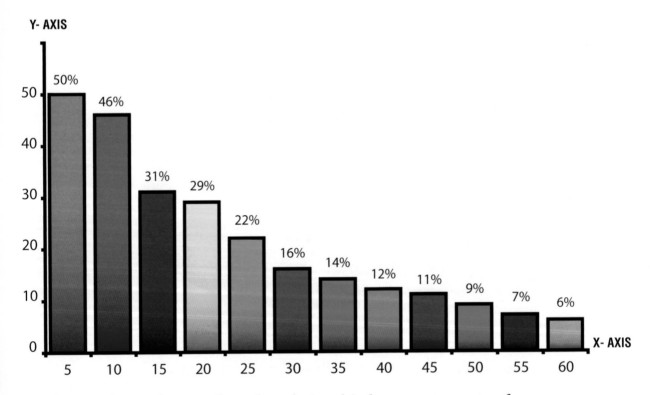

This graph uses bars to show the relationship between two sets of numbers. According to the graph, which value on the y-axis is equal to 25 on the x-axis?

Reading a Graph

This graph shows the relationship between time and the people who have had to leave their homes due to war and natural disaster. The x-axis shows the number of people, while the y-axis shows the year.

How many people left their homes in 1981? Run a finger across the grid from the year "1981" on the y-axis until it reaches the end of the bar on the x-axis. Then, run your finger up from the x-axis until it meets the point you found on the y-axis. What is the value of "x"? This is the number of people.

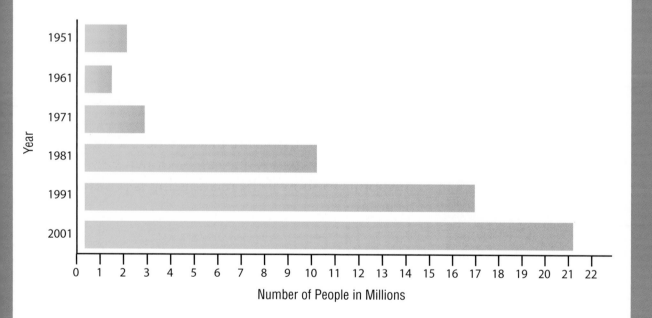

Answers: about 10 million

Knowing Types of Graphs

There are many types of graphs. Each shows information in a different way.

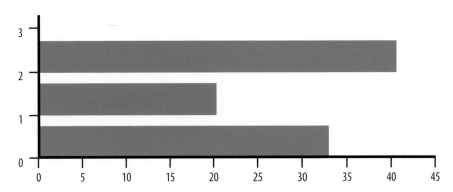

Bar Graphs
Bar graphs or line graphs are used to compare things. They have vertical or horizontal bars or lines to show information. The larger the value, the taller or longer the bar will be on the graph. A bar or line that has a value of 20 will be twice as tall or long as a bar or line that has a value of 10.

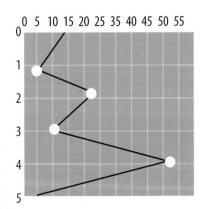

Scatter Plots
On a scatter plot, dots are placed where the x-axis relates to the y-axis. A line can be drawn between the points to show if the relationship is positive or negative.

Pictographs
Pictographs use symbols or pictures to compare variables on the axis. For example, stars may be used to show how many students in each grade earned above average scores on a test.

Identifying the Graph

Look at the graphs on this page. Can you tell which are bar graphs, scatter plots, or pictographs? Do you think the graph is best suited to the data shown? What other type of graph could be used to show the same information well?

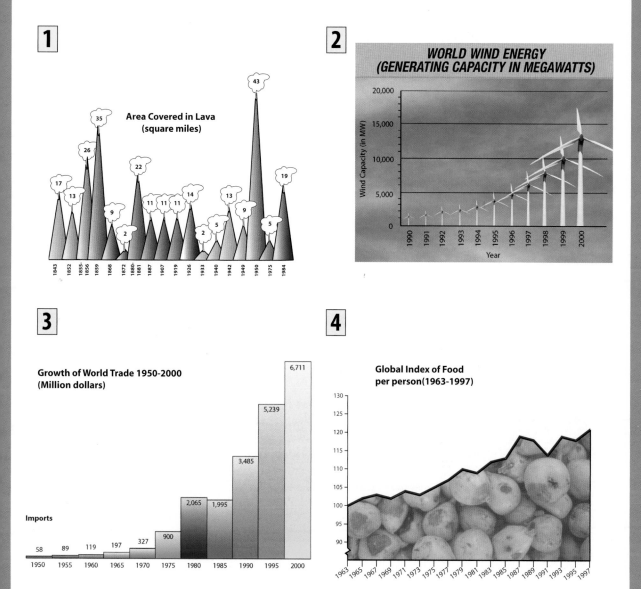

1

Area Covered in Lava
(square miles)

2

WORLD WIND ENERGY
(GENERATING CAPACITY IN MEGAWATTS)

3

Growth of World Trade 1950-2000
(Million dollars)

Imports

4

Global Index of Food
per person (1963-1997)

Answers: 1.) pictograph 2.) pictograph 3.) bar graph 4.) scatter plot

Using Graphs

A graph should be properly labeled. The topic of the variables and the values of the items being compared should be listed on the axes. The graph should be accurate. It should clearly show the correct information and have a title.

If a graph is well made, it will help the reader easily understand the data. A good graph will help explain ideas in a way that is factual and clear. It should be free from extra items. This way the graph can be read and understood quickly.

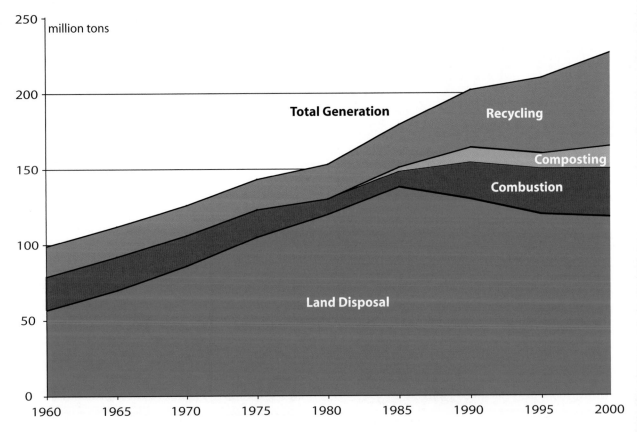

This graph shows the way waste has been disposed of in the United States over time.

Making a Graph

Use the information in this chart to make a graph that compares the distance traveled to the cost of the trip. First, think about which type of graph will best show the information you want to present.

Make a practice graph. You may want to use a different color for each type of vehicle. Be sure to include a legend showing what the colors represent.

Show the graph to your friends or family. Ask them if they understand the information on the graph. Then, make any corrections or changes that are needed, and draw your final graph.

TAKE THE TRAIN

For short trips between cities, taking the train can be faster and cheaper than driving, or even flying.

The chart below compares the cost and travel time of three trips by train, car, and plane. Travel time includes the time it takes to get to the station or airport and board the train or plane.

TRIP	DISTANCE	TRAIN	CAR	PLANE
San Diego, CA, to Los Angeles, CA	130 miles (209 km)	Time 2:45 $13	Time 2:24 $25–$62	Time 2:30 $152–$546
Chicago, IL, to Milwaukee, WI	90 miles (145 km)	Time 1:40 $19	Time 1:50 $18–$45	Time 2:30 $122–$262
New York, NY, to Albany, NY	156 miles (251 km)	Time 2:30 $33	Time 3:12 $32–$78	Time 3:30 $175–$255

Other Types of Graphs

Area Graphs

Area graphs can be used to show how something changes over time. Like other graphs, area graphs have an x-axis and a y-axis. Usually, the x-axis has numbers for a time period, and the y-axis has numbers for what is being measured. Area graphs can be used when organizing data that is constantly changing or has been collected in a short time period.

Area graphs often use shaded areas to display their information. This can give the graph a **three-dimensional** look. These graphs sometimes use a legend to explain what each shaded area represents.

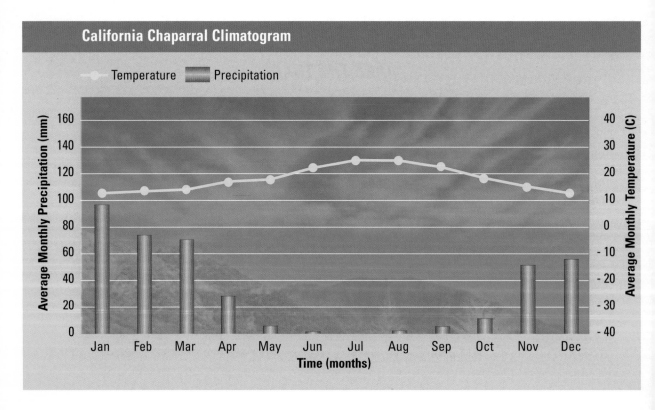

Look at this chart. It uses both scatter plots and bars to show different kinds of information on one area graph.

Making an Area Graph

Make your own area graph. Begin by making a chart called "Pets My Classmates Have." Ask your classmates what kinds of pets they have. Then, write down the types of pets and the number each of your classmates has. Add up the total for each type of pet.

Next, make a graph. Along the x-axis, list the types of pets, such as dogs, cats, and rabbits. Write the numbers 1 through 8 on the y-axis. Then, make an area graph that shows how the types of pets compare to the total for each type. Shade in the area below the lines you have drawn on the graph.

Dog

Birds

Fish

Cat

Put Your Knowledge To Use

Now that you know how to use charts and graphs, you can create your own. Begin by making a survey for your friends and family. First, select a topic you would like to know more about. Then, form a question about your topic. Think of five possible answers to your question. Ask your friends which one of the five answers they think best answers the question.

Once you have the answers to your questions, create a chart. In one column, write the possible answers. Along the top, write the numbers zero through five. Then, put the number of times people selected each answer in the correct column. Now, make a graph using your answers. The following is an example.

What food would you like to have served in the cafeteria at lunch?						
Votes	0	1	2	3	4	5
Cheeseburgers	X					
Pizzas				X		
Salad			X			
Lasagna						X
Sub sandwiches		X				

Websites for Further Research

Many books and websites provide information on charts and graphs. To learn more about charts and graphs, borrow books from the library, or surf the Internet.

To learn more about creating graphs, visit http://nces.ed.gov/nceskids/createagraph

To find out more about charts and graphs, go to http://42explore.com/graphs.htm

To learn how to read charts and graphs, visit www.tv411.org/index.shtml. Click on "Reading," and then on "Reading Charts and Graphs."

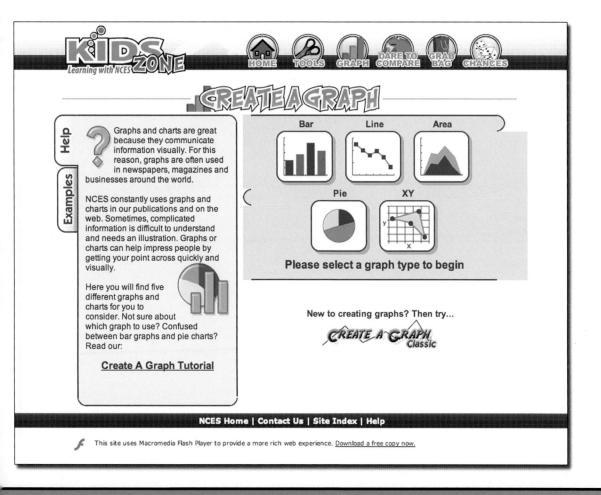

Glossary

axes: two reference lines that measure coordinates

baleen: an elastic, hornlike substance grown from the roof of the mouth of some whales

cetaceans: a group of marine mammals that has a horizontal tail fin and a blowhole for breathing

data: facts collected together for reference

graphic organizers: visual representations of information

three-dimensional: showing width, depth, and height

variables: uncertainties

Index